YOUR KNOWLEDGE HAS VALUE

Iramba Iramba

Learning experiences through coperative learning and teaching methods

GRIN Verlag

Bibliografische Information der Deutschen Nationalbibliothek:

Die Deutsche Bibliothek verzeichnet diese Publikation in der Deutschen National-
bibliografie; detaillierte bibliografische Daten sind im Internet über http://dnb.d-
nb.de/ abrufbar.

Imprint:

Copyright © 2012 GRIN Verlag GmbH
Druck und Bindung: Books on Demand GmbH, Norderstedt Germany
ISBN: 978-3-656-34243-4

This book at GRIN:

http://www.grin.com/en/e-book/207111/learning-experiences-through-coperative-
learning-and-teaching-methods

LEARNING EXPERIENCES THROUGH COOPERATIVE LEARNING AND TEACHING METHODS

Iramba Freddie Warioba Iramba

Department of Educational Management and Policy Studies
College of Education, University of Dodoma

INTRODUCTION

Cooperative Learning has been recommended and mandated as the most useful teaching and learning method by the Ministry of Education and Vocational Training in Tanzania. Perhaps, operating in consistence with the challenges of learner-centred education, the ministry came out with the Teacher Education Programme (TEP) as a professional support to college tutors. Most instructors of teachers colleges in Tanzania have taken the TEP which emphasizes the learner- centred ideology; a paradigm shift away from the traditional teacher-centred education. Capitalizing on quantitative and qualitatative data, this paper makes a critical reflection on the learning experiences through cooperative teaching methods in Tanzania primary schools. The paper is divided into five parts. The first part examines cooperative learning as a learner- centred activity. The second part explores both the roles of teachers and students in a cooperative teaching and learning setting. The third part highlights the measured learning effects through cooperative teaching methods. The fourth part is the author's reflections on his learning experiences through Cooperative Learning and Teaching Methods. The fifth part is a conclusion of the paper.

Cooperative Learning: a learner-centred activity

It was Vygotsky who first approached the idea of cooperative learning as an important tool in developing a child's cognitive process. According to Santrock (2004), Vygotsky's idea of knowledge is that "it is not generated from within the individual but rather is constructed through interaction with other people and objects in the culture." The idea of cooperative learning stems from the works of Lev Vygotsky, but what is exactly Cooperative learning? Cooperative learning is the learning process done in a setting where children help each other in understanding and internalizing subjects in a way that learning can help in an easier way, and in a child's own terms (Webb, Troper, & Fall 1995). (Peer discourse provides speakers with an opportunity to integrate their ideas while speaking, and listeners may receive new information that helps them construct new ideas." (Chin, O'Donnell & Jinks 2000) Also, according to Blumenfeld et al. (1996), Cooperative learning works when "successful groups promote (a) student exchanges that enhance reasoning and

1

higher-order thinking; (b) cognitive processing such as rehearsing, organizing, and integrating information; (c) perspective-taking and accommodation to others' ideas; and (d) acceptance and encouragement among those involved with the work."

It is important to notice that it is not any interaction that will provide a positive cooperative learning experience. On the contrary, cooperative activities must be well organized, and supervised by a teacher who is aware of how to work with the cooperative perspective. Indeed, "learning from peers in cooperative or collaborative groups is complex and difficult to achieve." (Blemenfeld et al. 1996). The more organized the setting are, the better is the outcome from such experience. Children are supposed to discuss the issues presented in an organized way, verbalizing as such as possible. Another point important in discussing and verbalizing, as a way to positively implement cooperative learning is the fact that "giving explanations is extremely beneficial to students … The quality of explanations given by an individual during group interaction is predictive of outcomes from that interaction." (Chinn, O'Donnell & Jinks, 2000). However, these explanations should occur in the right moment, serving as a crucial tool in understanding. The child who gives explanation should do so in a way it is pertinent to the subject, and also in a lingo that can be understood by peers. (Webb, Troper & Fall, 1995).

Roles of a teacher and Students in Cooperative Learning and Teaching

Giving ideas or new results to the task enables a child to think in an organized manner, and allows other students to understand matters in their own way, reflect on what was said, and put that in the subject's perspective in order to finish the activity in a positive way. "One important and robust finding is that giving explanations is extremely beneficial to students. (Also,) the quality of explanations given by an individual during group interaction is predictive of outcomes from that interaction." (Chinn, O'Donnell & Jinks, 2000).

In order for discussion between students to happen, it is important to have a mediator who is for the implementation of cooperative activities. Here where the teacher's role becomes crucial in successfully implementing cooperative activities in the classroom. First of all, it is necessary for teacher to not only be interested in the cooperative approach, but also to be well aware on how to put it in practice. Welch (1998) views cooperative approach as a collaborative activity and contends that:

2

Teacher education programs must consider developing courses and field experiences that introduce principles of collaboration … Teacher education programs must provide a foundation for collaboration, including exploration of various theoretical constructs and definitions of collaboration. This exploration should encompass a variety of disciplinary perspective, including systems/organizational theory and sociological concepts.

It is important that teachers come prepared to class when using cooperative approach or activities. One of the problems teachers might encounter is the fact that, since cooperative activities demand extra attention, they might fall behind with the curriculum, and this is a concern of most teachers. Another problem can be in what concerns in putting extra effort in succeeding with the cooperative method, once it needs constant attention. (Nath, Ross & Smith, 1996).

Once the teachers are in the classroom environment, and want to use cooperative activities, it is necessary that the teacher works as a mediator and a facilitator in creating the best environment for the method. First of all, the teacher must separate the class in groups, and within this group, he or she must allocate students who will not overcome one another while in the activity. Therefore, groups should be assigned with students of both genders, different ethnicities, and also based on their cognitive skills. (Sapon-Shevin & Schniedewind, 2001). According to Nath and Ross (2001), "students with higher reading assessment scores were coupled with students having lower reading assessment scores." Indeed, "learning from peers in cooperative or collaborative groups is complex and difficult to achieve." (Blumenfeld etal. 1996) and it is up to the teacher to make sure that students will be able to get as much information as possible from others students within their groups.

Another important task for a teacher is to inform students on what concerns a cooperative activity. (Research has shown that teaching students how to elaborate or reason, for example by teaching 'ground rules' for cooperation, can have a positive effect on peer interaction in cooperative activities." (Staarman & Krol, 2005). In preparing students to perform in cooperative activities, teachers are working on the betterment of the activity. With more defined paths to follow, the definition on the roles of students becomes easier as well.

By enabling students to experience cooperatively structured learning in a cooperative classroom, teacher provides them the experimental knowledge that democracy, care for others, shared power, respect for diversity, collective success, and positive interdependence are viable, valuable, and meaningful ways to live together. Sapon-Shevin & Schniedewind, 2001).

Students in a cooperative environment work together in order to have the whole group to generate an alternative end that is beneficial and understandable to all members. (Gamson 1994) The level of interaction is as great as possible, and students work together, as their own teachers. As it was previously mentioned, students help each other understand issues in their own language; this way, children can work together and instruct each other in explaining situations, given new ideas for outcomes, as well as "students disagreeing constructively, praising one another, encouraging one another, and (most importantly) using low voices." (Nath, Ross & Smith 1996).

According to Webb, Troper & Fall (1995), the exchange of information can be useful for both students; the one who talks, and the one who listens; moreover:

> A primary motivation for putting students into groups is the opportunity for student to help each other learn. Students can help each other learn by giving and receiving help; by recognizing contradictions between their own and other students' perspectives, seeking new knowledge to resolve those contradictions, and constructing new understanding from them; and by internalizing problem solving processes and strategies that other students use or that are created jointly with others.

In the classroom environment, it is commonly found different types of students: the ones who are the leaders of the class, the ones who follow the leaders, and the ones who do not engage in many relationships, in cooperative activities, all these different types of students meet, in order to exchange as much experience as possible. These students are put in situations where they need to work together, and for that, several elements need to be present in the interaction. Students must talk to one another, and this should happen in the form of dialogue, never raising their voices, and taking turns as they speak. Also, there must be some sharing of the task, with students doing things dependently of each other. If any disagreement occurs, discussion must happen in the most respectful way, and aiming at a solution to the problem. In addition, students are asked to help each other to the most, explaining in case of doubts, and encouraging others in case of disappointments. (Nath & Ross, 2001)

One last issue very important in implementing cooperative activities in the classroom environment is the role of the school as a whole. Not only teacher and students play an important part in making the cooperative methods to work, but also the school, and people behind it, plays an important part. The school head, for instance, is crucial in reinforcing the methods to teachers, and encouraging them to act them. Other teachers can also work together in order to help each other in answering any questions or doubts that might come across a teacher's way. In a study made by Nath, Ross & Smith (1996), the role of the school head was vital for the continuation of the experiment, and had a strong impression throughout the study that the school head served a critical role in maintaining the school wide cooperative learning initiative and that the school continually provided encouragement."

Measured Learning Effects:

Cooperative approach is a topic of much discussion. Mostly because although theorists believe that the method is extremely beneficial for children, quantitative data show quite the opposite result. Most of the measured information on cooperative learning has negatives outcomes for activities using the method. However, some studies actually showed that if the activity is guided properly, then the outcomes can be more favorable.

In a study lead by Nath, & Smith (1996), the research showed that positive and negative aspects were seen in a cooperative environment:

> Teachers also indicated that students were more enthusiastic toward learning using STAD (Students Teams-Achievement Divisions) than when doing individualized work ... From semester 1 and 2 increases were found in the percentage of teachers who agreed that STAD had a positive impact on students communication and social skills (78% to 100%) and on achievement (67% to 78%).

However, some students were noticed not interacting properly, or even not interacting at all. Another problem with this study was that some children would prefer to work alone and also that students were simply not old enough to fully understand the method.

A similar problem was shown on a research made by Staarman & Krol (2005), where it was noticed some differences in group productivity according to the age: " In general compared to grade six students, students in grade four have developed less knowledge and skills on several domains" This only emphasizes how ineffective cooperative learning can be for children. Even though the research showed that there were some issues that could have been improved in performing the research, still, the general outcomes shows that children of a young age are simply not prepared for such activity.

5

An experiment made by Barclay & Breheny (1994) shows the opposite result, and even discusses the age problem. In the experiment, kindergarten children were asked to perform in a cooperative activity where they would decide what would be learned, and how the topic would be learned. This study had the children first pick out the next topic to be researched, and then the process in which children did their researches, with the help of others, and the final outcome. Impressively, kindergarten children showed organization, and responsibility in completing the task. The students were interested and the research was a success. Of course, children had the cooperation or collaboration of some adults, in order to monitor how the task would be performed, but children did most of the work by themselves. "Also, we recognize the importance of having the support and involvement of parents, classroom volunteers, and 'buddies.' Without this outside help, the project would need to conduct over a longer period of time."

To increase the discussion on cooperative learning, another research on the method made by Nath & Ross (2001) showed some interesting aspects that agree with the results of Barclay & Breheny mentioned above on what concerns age students: "An unexpected finding was that the grade 1 and 3 students performed better in cooperative grouping than grade 4 – 6 students." Still, the study does not clarify on how effective cooperative learning really is since "both quantitative and qualitative analyses suggested that peer-tutoring training generally but not consistently enhanced student communication and collaborative skills."

Cooperative learning when quantitatively measured shows some conflict on whether it is effective or not. The number of positive outcomes is small, and even those are noted of having some minor problems in certain aspects. However, many educators still insist in using the system as a way for children to learn.

Reflections on Learning Experiences through Cooperative Learning and Teaching

Methods

To finish this paper I would like to add some of my own experiences in using the cooperative method in learning. My primary school years were in a school where cooperation was part of class in probably seventy percent of the time, and children interacted most of the day in activities that ranged from mathematical problems to a simple collage of pictures. First, I would like to describe the classroom set up, and then talk about some of my experiences, to later give some feedback on my experiences once young of the cooperative perspective.

The school was a small government establishment, in a rural area in Bunda District in Tanzania. The classroom was made of one teacher, and pupils ranging from twenty to thirty per class. Each school day, the pupils would be separated in different small groups made up of three, four or five pupils split into different areas of the room. There was no separate desks; instead, children were made to sit on the desks placed around tables with different shapes (circle, square, or rectangular), and were entitled different group names (usually the name would correspond to alphabetical letters or names of wild animals). Pupils would work together for most part of the day, except for the reading portion.

The day class was divided into periods. When Maths period began, pupils would refer to it as "Math period and so on. Each pupil would have their own materials (slates, pencils, paper, etc.) in order to diminish any difference between pupils. Also, boys and girls were grouped together, and there was no order of how the separation would take place. By the end of the year, each pupil would at least interact with all pupils in class.

Children were very participative in all activities,. Especially in the writing portions of class. Pupils in the same group would help each other in spelling, and also in how to write the letter in the right way. Another section of class where interaction levels were high was during Maths period (adding, subtracting, multiplication, division, etc). In this portion of class, contact between pupils was also very high, and children would have long discussions on how to find the answer. Note here that this is the type of cooperative learning so discussed, and so aimed by many researchers. Children in my class discussing how to find the best outcome, giving each other explanation, and simply trading experience and thoughts.

By the time I left this school, and went to a secondary school, which focused more on individual work, I sometimes felt unprepared. I would have moments of doubts, thinking I was simply not prepared for the type of school most children my age were used to. But when the time to be tested would come, I would always succeed. My school had been able to prepare me for the future, but in a way that curriculum never felt as an obligation. On the contrary, time spent in my primary school went by fast, and the feelings I have nowadays is that we learned without even noticing that we were doing so.

Conclusion

The cooperative methods change the way learners experience subjects, and the results are only being noticed as a child grows up. Maybe in the quantitative measurement, the results are discouraging, but in a broader picture, cooperative methods in teaching children are well worth and valuable for the rest of the child's life. It is necessary for teachers to have the patience. knowledge and tools in order to promote it properly amidst the many challenges posed by the approach but once in practice, makes a great difference for all members in the school setup.

References

Abbeduto, L. (2004). **Is Cooperative Learning Effective**? *Taking Sides-Clashing View on* Controversial Issues in Education Psychology (pp. 300-319). Wisconsin State, Publisher McGraw-Hill.

Barclay, K. & Breheny, C. (1994). **Letting the Children Take Over More of their Own Learning Collaborative Research in Kindergarten Classroom**. *Young Children, 49(6)*, 33-39.

Blumenfeld, P., Marx, R., Soloway, E., & Krajcik, J. (1996). **Learning With Peers: From Small Group Cooperation to Collaborative Communities**. *Educational Researcher,25(8)*, 37-40.

Chinn, C., O'Donnell, A., & Jinks, T. (2000). **The Structure of Discourse in Collaborative Learning**. *The Journal of Experimental Education, 69(1)*, 77-97.

Gamson, Z. (1994). **Collaborative Learning Comes of Age**. *Change, 26*, 44-49.

Keedy, J. & Drmacich, D. (1994). **The Collaborative Curriculum at the School Without Walls: Empowering Students for Classroom Learning**. *The Urban review, 26(2)*, 121-135.

Nath, L., & Ross, S. (2001). **The Influence of a Peer-Tutoring Training Mode for Cooperative Grouping With Elementary Students**. *ETR&D, 29(2)*, 41-56.

Nath, L., Ross, S., & Smith, L. (1996). **A case Study of implementing a Cooperative Learning Program in an Inner-City School**. *The Journal of Experimental Educational, 64(2),*117-136.

Santrock, J. (2004). *Child Development*. New York, NY: McGraw-Hill.

Sapon-Shevin, M., & Schniedewind, N. (1992). **If Cooperative Learning is the Answer, What are the Questions**? Journal of Education, 174(2), 11-37.

Staarman, J., & Krol, K. (2005). **Peer Interaction in Three Collaborative Learning Environment**s, *Journal of Classroom Interaction, 40(1)*, 29-39.

Webb, N., Trope, J., & Fall, R. (1995). **Constructive Activity and Learning in Collaborative Small Groups**. *Journal of Educational Psychology, 87(3)*, 406-423.

Welch, M. (1998). **Collaboration: Staying on the Bandwagon**. *Journal of Teacher Education, 49(1)*, 26-37.